THE
UNITED STATES
HOLOCAUST
MEMORIAL
MUSEUM

AMERICA KEEPS THE MEMORY ALIVE

THE
UNITED STATES
HOLOCAUST
MEMORIAL
MUSEUM

AMERICA KEEPS THE MEMORY ALIVE

by Eleanor H. Ayer

 **DILLON PRESS**
New York

Maxwell Macmillan Canada
Toronto

Maxwell Macmillan International
New York   Oxford   Singapore   Sydney

In memory of the millions who perished . . .
And in tribute to my friend Helen Waterford,
whose story is preserved at the Museum.
May her belief in bearing no hatred or vengeance
stand as an inspiration to us all.

Acknowledgments

My sincere thanks to several staff members at the United States Holocaust Memorial Museum, for helping to ensure the accuracy of the text and for assisting in acquiring photographs. Specifically they are Dr. Michael Berenbaum, director of research; Ms. Naomi Paiss, director of communications; Ms. Susan Morgen-stein, director of exhibitions; Ms. Beth Redlich, coordinator of photographic services; Ms. Genya Markon, head of photo archives.

—EHA

Photo Credits

Cover: courtesy Robert C. Lautman, © 1993.
© Stadarchiv Nurnberg: 22. Alan Gilbert/USHMM: 8, 12, 16, 20, 24, 30, 38, 43, 52, 74. Arnold Kramer/USHMM: 35, 45, 49. Ed Owen/USHMM: 14, 42, 54. USHMM: 41, 47, 52, 54, 56, 57, 65, 68, 70, 71

Book design by Carol Matsuyama

Library of Congress Cataloging-in-Publication Data

Ayer, Eleanor, H.
    The United States Holocaust Memorial Museum : America keeps the memory alive / by Eleanor H. Ayer.
       p. cm.
    Includes bibliographical references and index.
    ISBN 0-87518-649-1   ISBN 0-382-24728-0 (pbk)
    1. U.S. Holocaust Memorial Museum—Juvenile literature. 2. Holocaust, Jewish (1939-1945)—Juvenile literature. I. Title.
D804.3.A97 1994
940.53'18'07473—dc20   94-4585

A description of the United States Holocaust Memorial Museum in Washington, D.C. The story of the Holocaust is interwoven with a Museum tour.

Dillon Press   Maxwell Macmillan Canada, Inc.
Macmillan Publishing Company   1200 Eglinton Avenue East
866 Third Avenue   Suite 200
New York, NY 10022   Don Mills, Ontario M3C 3N1

Macmillan Publishing Company is part of the Maxwell Communication Group of Companies.

First edition

Printed in the United States of America

10 9 8 7 6 5 4 3 2 1

CONTENTS

CONCOURSE LEVEL

"FOR THE DEAD AND THE LIVING, WE MUST BEAR WITNESS"

The picture on the square ceramic tile is a yellow Star of David, the six-pointed symbol of Judaism. Painted over the star is a simple question, *Where Is God?* It is a question the Jews of Europe asked themselves many times during the years 1933–1945, when hatred inflamed the world and millions of people were killed without cause.

This tile is one of 3,300 painted by American middle school students in the 1980s. They were studying the Holocaust—the intentional murder of six million Jews, planned and carried out by Germany's Nazi government and its supporters during World War II. The Holocaust began with the Jews, but, before it was over, another five million innocent people had been killed by Adolf Hitler and his Nazi followers. Among them were Roma (Gypsies), Jehovah's Witnesses, communists and political prisoners, homosexuals, and the handicapped.

After learning about the horrors of the Holocaust, the children painted their thoughts on the tiles. One shows a large, black swastika—the Nazi symbol—in a red circle with a slash across it. Another is a painting of tiny teardrops, with the title *Tears of Death*. There is a Star of David painted in barbed

7

wire, like that used to fence in prisoners at the death camps of Nazi Europe. Other tiles have only words: *The Hurt Still Lives* and *Children Need Love and Friends.*

The ceramic tiles hang today in the United States Holocaust Memorial Museum in Washington, D.C. Above them, across a long wall, is a message reminding visitors that of the six million Jews who died in the Holocaust, approximately one and a half million were children. Workers were

Some of the 3,300 tiles that make up the Wall of Remembrance, on the Museum's Concourse Level.

still mounting the letters of this message above the tiles as the first visitors entered the Museum in April 1993: *The First to Perish Were the Children. . . . From These the New Dawn Might Have Risen.*

Many of the tiles use the words *Never Again* or *Never Forget* as part of their design. The wall where they are mounted—on the lower, or Concourse, level of the Museum—is called the Wall of Remembrance. To remember, *Never to Forget, Ever,* is a major theme of the Holocaust Memorial Museum. Its creators hope that the flames of the Holocaust will burn in people's minds forever, as a reminder of the depths to which humankind can sink. Keeping these memories alive may help to ensure that another Holocaust is never allowed to happen.

The Holocaust: The blackest hour in modern history

The events that the Museum commemorates began in Europe in 1933, when Adolf Hitler became the chancellor of Germany. The country had suffered a devastating defeat in World War I. Since then, thousands of its citizens had been out of work, hungry, and discouraged. They saw Hitler as a savior who could lead them out of poverty and make their nation mighty once again.

But the new *Führer*, as Germany called its leader, harbored a burning hatred that would eventually consume him, along with much of Europe. Hitler was an anti-Semite: He hated Jews. In his autobiography, *Mein Kampf (My Struggle)*, he called Jews "snakes," "vermin," "parasites," "maggots," and a host of other vile names. Yet *Mein Kampf* became the bible of the National Socialist German Workers' Party—the Nazis.

In his book, Hitler blamed the Jews for Germany's defeat in World War I, saying the war might not have been lost "if some twelve or fifteen thousand of the Hebrew corrupters of the people had been poisoned by gas before or during the war." It was a frightening prophecy of what was soon to come.

Hitler's goal was to build a "Master Race" of what he considered to be true, pure Germans. These "Aryans," as he called them, would preferably have blond hair and blue eyes, although many native Germans had dark hair and eyes. This "Aryan" race would be superior to all others, and would show no trace of Jewish or Gypsy blood.

Hitler planned to reunite people of Germanic backgrounds from around the world and bring them together under his government of National Socialism. To ensure that the Master Race had enough territory, Hitler began seeking *Lebensraum*, or "living space." In 1938, German army troops marched first into Austria and then into Czechoslovakia, overtaking both countries in quick and bloodless victories. A year later, on September 1, 1939, in a move that sparked the outbreak of World War II, Hitler invaded Poland. Soon that country was also defeated, and parts of it were joined to the growing German Third Reich, as Hitler called the empire he hoped to create. Having conquered Poland, Hitler proclaimed loudly to world leaders that he would seek no new territory. But this claim was a lie, like so many others he made while in power. The Nazi military machine rolled on to overtake much of Europe, as well as parts of Asia and Africa.

Under cover of war, a more bizarre and one-sided battle was taking place. This was Hitler's war against the Jews and other *Untermenschen*—the inferior people. What Nazi leaders

10

were planning was genocide—the intentional murder of an entire race of people. Although they eventually would lose World War II, Hitler and his followers would very nearly win the war against the Jews.

Why was the Holocaust allowed to happen?

Why didn't anyone stop Hitler and the Nazis from carrying out their plan of genocide? Some people did try, but there were far too few of them. One was Varian Fry, an American journalist working in wartime France. Fry's heroic efforts to rescue thousands of people from the *Gestapo*, the much-feared Nazi secret police, are remembered in an exhibit titled "Assignment Rescue," on the Concourse level of the Holocaust Museum.

Another hero of the Holocaust was a Swedish diplomat to Hungary, Raoul Wallenberg. Hungary's large Jewish population was in great peril after German troops overtook the country in March 1944. Using his influence as a diplomat, Wallenberg had thousands of Swedish "safe passes" printed, which he gave to the Jews. Since Sweden was a neutral country, Jews in Hungary were safe as Swedish "citizens." In this way, Wallenberg saved the lives of perhaps as many as 70,000 people. To honor his heroism, the street on which the Holocaust Museum is located in Washington, D.C., has been renamed Raoul Wallenberg Place.

There also were heroes among ordinary people, and they, too, are remembered at the Museum. Many of them were Gentiles—non-Jews—who were appalled by the Nazis' torture and murder of innocent people. At great peril to themselves and their families, they hid Jews in their homes, stole

The United States Holocaust Memorial Museum on Raoul Wallenberg Place in Washington, D.C. The white, six-sided building in the foreground is the Hall of Remembrance. Behind it is the main museum building, its eight towers reminiscent of guard stations in Nazi concentration camps.

food coupons so the Jews could eat, and protected them against discovery and deportation by the Gestapo. Thanks to the efforts of these people, thousands of lives were saved.

But although their efforts were great, their numbers were small. Millions of victims might not have died in the Holocaust had more people opened their eyes to the Nazis and opened their hearts to their fellow citizens. As you tour the Museum exhibits, you cannot help but ask, "What would I have done?" If you had been alive during the Holocaust, would you have helped to hide a Jew, even if doing so meant possible death to you and your family? Or would you have taken the safer route and looked the other way when the Gestapo hauled your neighbor off to a prison camp?

"Never to forget, ever"

At the dedication of the United States Holocaust Memorial Museum, speaker Elie Wiesel, a death camp survivor and winner of the Nobel Peace Prize, asked: "How could the murderers do what they did and go on living? Why was there no public outcry?" The Museum does not answer these questions, he explained, because there are no answers. The Museum's purpose is to keep these questions alive in people's minds, so that we never, ever forget what can happen when we close our eyes to our fellow human beings. Said Israeli President Chaim Herzog, another speaker at the dedication, "It is not enough to have justice on your side. You must stand up and defend it."

At the close of the ceremony, U.S. President Bill Clinton lit an eternal flame, in memory of the victims of the Holocaust, which would stand as a sentinel to future generations. As he lit the flame, Clinton reminded people that the Museum was not a memorial "for the dead alone, or for the survivors. Most of all it is for those of us who were not there. . . . We will be forever strengthened by remembrance."

Why America?

Why was the Museum—a memorial to the Holocaust, which happened in Europe—built in the United States? Some critics say it should not have been located in Washington, surrounded by pillars to American achievement like the Washington Monument, the Jefferson and Lincoln Memorials, and the Smithsonian Institution.

But the Holocaust was not just a European problem. It is a scar on all humankind. It is a burden that each of us must bear and a warning that all of us should heed. If we fail to

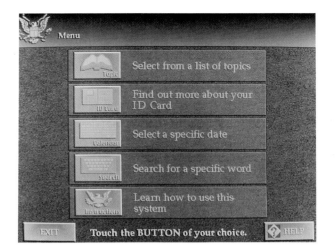

Computer menu for accessing information about the Holocaust, located in the Wexner Learning Center, on the Museum's second floor.

learn from the lessons of the past, another Holocaust could happen—right here in America, the cradle of freedom. The United States, as a guardian of democracy, has a responsibility to remind the world of the importance of every person's rights. For those reasons, it is fitting that the Holocaust Museum is located in the heart of the country that represents those freedoms and rights.

The Museum's primary purpose is to teach. Its goal is to educate visitors, as well as students around the country, about the facts of the Holocaust, the conditions that allowed such hatred to grow, and the horror that it inflicted on the world. It is hoped that by understanding the facts, people will become more understanding of each other, and thus will prevent such an explosion of hatred from ever happening again.

Harvey Meyerhoff, one of the Museum's founders, says its purpose is to teach about bigotry, hatred, and intolerance. "This Museum," he said at the dedication, "remembers events which never should have been seen by human eyes, but having been seen must never be forgotten."

HALL
OF
WITNESS

As you enter the Hall of Witness to begin your tour of the Holocaust Museum, a message carved in black granite reminds you of why you are there. *You are my witness*, reads the quotation from the biblical book of Isaiah. You have an obligation to share with others the sobering lessons you will learn inside these walls.

The huge, skylit ceiling of the Hall of Witness is constructed of 304 glass panels. Outside, roof turrets resemble the guard towers atop the concentration camps where the Nazis imprisoned their victims. Architect James Freed, who designed the Holocaust Museum, visited the remains of concentration camps in Europe. He came home knowing that the Museum buildings must do more than house displays and artifacts. They must reflect the moods of anxiety, fear, and despair that enveloped the Jews of Europe during the Holocaust. "I wanted to convey the feeling of constantly being watched, of things closing in," said Freed.

The exposed steel beams that support the Hall of Witness help to deliver Freed's message. They are rough and harsh, like those inside a factory or warehouse. Rather than meeting at nice neat angles, they are deliberately skewed and irregular, to give visitors an uneasy, disruptive feeling—the same feeling that prisoners experienced at the concentration camps.

In the Hall of Witness is a stairway leading to the exhibit floors in the Museum. The stairs are tapered as they rise,

Steel beams support the skylit roof of the Hall of Witness. Stairs leading to the second floor resemble the railroad tracks leading into the death camp of Auschwitz-Birkenau.

16

looking eerily like the railroad tracks that led into Auschwitz-Birkenau, the largest Nazi death camp in Poland. But visitors do not go up the stairs; they take an elevator to the fourth floor to begin their tour *down* through the Museum, just as the Nazis' victims descended into their human-made hell.

Before boarding the elevator, all visitors pick up an ID, or "Identity Card," to carry with them throughout the tour. On it is printed a short biography of a person who lived during the Holocaust. Some of the people on the ID cards survived; others perished.

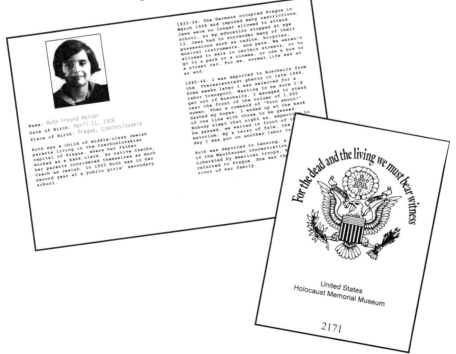

The Identity Card of Ruth Reiser, one of more than 500 profiles of Holocaust victims whose stories are told on ID cards at the Museum.

Thomas Pfeffer, from Amsterdam in the Netherlands, and Ruth Reiser, from Prague, Czechoslovakia, are two of 500 people whose stories are on the ID cards. Ruth, the daughter of a bank clerk, was seven years old when Hitler came to power in 1933. Tommy was born in the Netherlands in 1936, to a Dutch-Jewish mother and a German-Jewish father. Heinz, Tommy's father, had fled from Germany when his uncle was murdered by the Nazis in a concentration camp. The ID cards help visitors realize that the Holocaust was not an impersonal event in history, but something that happened to millions of real people, just like Tommy and Ruth.

3
FOURTH FLOOR

THE
NAZI ASSAULT,
1933–1939

Abarren elevator with steel-gray walls carries visitors to the fourth floor of the Museum to begin the tour. During the ride, a TV monitor plays a black-and-white newsreel film of American soldiers freeing prisoners in the concentration camps at the end of World War II. The soldiers' voices say that they cannot believe what their eyes are seeing. All around them are hundreds of dead and dying prisoners.

While the film is still running, the elevator opens onto a darkened wall with bold, foot-high letters: **THE HOLOCAUST**. Beside the words is a huge photo of a concentration camp on liberation day, set on fire by the Nazis as they fled from the liberators. The charred logs of the buildings cannot be distinguished from the charred bodies of the prisoners who were left behind to perish in the inferno. Hanging near the photo is a blue-and-white striped uniform, like those worn by many inmates at the camps.

Having had a quick glimpse of the end, you now move backward in time to an exhibit titled "Before the Holocaust." On display are family photos covering the years 1900 to 1930, when Europe was home to nine million Jews. A chart shows

19

the percentage of Jews then living in each of the European countries. Poland had the largest percentage—nearly 10 percent of its citizens were Jewish. Romania also had a high count—nearly 750,000 Jews. Just twelve years after Hitler came to power, two out of every three European Jews would be dead.

The Nazis take control

A huge, intimidating photo of two SA guards looms ahead. The SA, or *Sturmabteilung*, the "storm troopers," was a radical branch of the Nazi army, powerful in the early days of Hitler's rule. By 1933 the SA—called Brownshirts for the

A fourth-floor display showing storm troopers holding a muzzled dog

color of their uniforms—had a half-million members. But as the Reich grew, another branch of the Nazi army became more powerful. This was the SS, or *Schutzstaffel*, the group that ran the concentration camps. One branch of the SS was the much-feared Gestapo, the secret police who hunted down Jews and other "undesirables" to fill the camps. The SA guards in this larger-than-life photo are leading a ferocious-looking German shepherd, muzzled and straining at its leash. The muzzles were attached in such a way that the SA could pull them off the dogs' mouths quickly, when the animals were needed to chase or attack a victim.

As you move past the displays showing how the Nazis gained a death grip on Germany, there is an unmistakable feeling of being herded along, just as prisoners were rounded up by the Gestapo. Signs and photos tell the story of the Nazi-ordered boycott of Jewish shops on April 1, 1933. ANYONE WHO BUYS FROM JEWS IS A TRAITOR! a sign warns. Photos show German store windows with the word *Jude* (Jew) painted across them in bold letters.

Next is a huge pile of discarded books, written by some of Europe's finest authors. Many of them were Jews or writers whose ideas did not follow Nazi teachings. On May 10, 1933, Nazi storm troopers and students at a Berlin university set fire to 35,000 such books. On the nearby glass panel is a quotation from Heinrich Heine, one of Germany's greatest poets, and among those whose writing was banned: *Where books are burned, in the end people will be burned.* Heine had been dead for more than seventy-five years when Hitler came to power, but he had chillingly foretold the future.

The Nazis had their own books and their own ideas of

German children reading The Poisonous Mushroom, *an anti-Semitic schoolbook*

what children should study in school. One of those displayed is a grossly anti-Semitic children's book titled *The Poisonous Mushroom*. On its cover is a large mushroom with a face in the center that is supposed to represent a "typical" Jewish man with a large nose.

Jews: The unwanted people

Ahead you see signs, printed in German, that were posted along village streets throughout the country during the 1930s and 1940s:

JEWS FORBIDDEN

JEWS ARE NOT WANTED IN THIS TOWN

22

Jews rapidly lost their rights in Nazi Germany, and on September 15, 1935, Hitler made it official: With the passage of the Nuremberg laws, all Jews lost their citizenship. They could no longer vote, hold public office, or fly the German flag. Jews were prohibited from marrying "Aryan" Germans. Advertisements clearly show how businesses discriminated against them. A brochure from a hotel of the day asks "guests of the Jewish race" to eat their meals in their rooms. Signs on park benches and in other public places read, FOR ARYANS ONLY or JEWS AND DOGS NOT PERMITTED.

In the schools, German children studied "racial science," a subject in which they learned how the Nazis supposedly told a Jew from an "Aryan" German. The Museum has a collection of tools used by "doctors" to determine just who was a Jew. There are calipers for measuring the size of a person's skull or the length of the nose, and charts for determining "Jewish" hair and eye color. Nearby is a very early data processing machine, made by the German division of IBM, in which statistics on Jews were entered and stored in card files.

The outlook for the Jews of Germany was grim. But it became bleak for Jews throughout the rest of Europe as well in March 1938, when German armies swept into Austria and Czechoslovakia. In the Museum's exhibit "Expansion Without War," visitors learn how Hitler was able to overtake these countries without resistance. For Ruth Reiser, who was living in Prague when the Germans invaded Czechoslovakia, "Normal life came to an end. Jews were no longer allowed to attend school, so my education stopped at age thirteen. We weren't allowed to walk in certain streets, to go to a park or cinema, or use a bus or streetcar."

Suddenly your tour path is blocked by a huge horizontal pole with red and white stripes. **VIOLATED BORDER**, the sign reads. The pole marks the border between Germany and Poland. You don't know what to do. Should you climb over it? Go back? It's confusing, disorienting, almost frightening. In a very small way, you are feeling the kind of fear that the hunted people of Hitler's Reich experienced: nowhere to turn, no place to go, forced from your familiar route to follow a different path.

Across Germany, Jews by the thousands were finding

Torah scrolls, torn during Kristallnacht, November 9, 1938

themselves trapped, with nowhere to turn. By late 1938, worry and uncertainty filled every Jewish home, as families wondered just how far the Nazis would carry their persecution. On November 9, they got their answer. That night, *Kristallnacht*—"the Night of Broken Glass"—the Nazis unleashed a firestorm of hatred against the Jews. A few days earlier, seventeen-year-old Herschel Grynszpan had killed a German official in Paris. Herschel was wild with rage because the German government had deported his parents to Poland. The SS responded to the official's death by rounding up some thirty thousand Jewish men and shipping them to concentration camps. Across Germany, Nazi fanatics smashed thousands of windows and set fire to Jewish synagogues, stores, and homes. Salvaged from one of the synagogues and displayed at the Museum today is a small wooden ark holding a Torah, the first five books of the Hebrew Bible, written in Hebrew on parchment. This sacred scroll of Jewish law and wisdom was slashed during the savagery of Kristallnacht.

Forced to flee

This was not the first time hatred had threatened the Jews of Europe. In a fifteen-minute film on the history of anti-Semitism, visitors learn of many other times and places in which Jews were persecuted. In the 1930s, just as in earlier times, persecution sparked a revival of Jewish faith and culture. Instead of abandoning their faith, Jews flocked to the synagogues in greater numbers, and the movement to-ward Zionism—the establishment of a Jewish homeland in Palestine—gained strength.

Hitler's goal was not only to make Europe *judenrein*

("cleansed of Jews") but also to rid it of his political and intellectual enemies. As part of the plan, he exiled many prominent people, forcing them to leave the country. On a wall display in the Museum are the faces of some of these exiles—scientist Albert Einstein, author Thomas Mann, and theologian Paul Tillich—who fled their homeland to escape the Nazis. Of these three, only Einstein was Jewish.

But it wasn't just prominent people or Jews whom the Nazis wanted out of Europe. Communists, liberal "free thinkers," Jehovah's Witnesses, homosexuals, Gypsies—these were some of Hitler's other victims who also lived in mortal fear of their government. Maria Sava Moise, whose story is told on an ID card, was a Romanian Gypsy who turned fourteen in 1939. Maria's family was too poor to send the children to school, so they worked with their mother, picking grapes for a local winery. Her father earned money by singing, as did many Gypsies. On display is a violin used by these wandering singers, along with some of their colorful clothes, and a cart like many Gypsies pulled as they traveled from place to place.

Some of the hunted people tried to flee, *if* they could find a country to take them in. Unfortunately most governments had quotas—limits on the numbers of migrants they would accept. Fearful of increasing the problems in their own countries, few leaders would change their quotas to admit more refugees. Despite its reputation as a haven for the persecuted, the United States was among those countries that refused to raise its quotas.

The Museum tells the sad story of the ship *St. Louis*, which left the German port of Hamburg in 1939, bound for Cuba. On board were 936 refugees, nearly all of them Jewish.

Maria Sava Moise

When the *St. Louis* pulled into Havana, the Cuban government refused to accept its passengers. Colombia, Chile, Paraguay, Argentina, and the United States also said no. So back to Europe the *St. Louis* sailed. Finally Belgium, the Netherlands, Britain, and France each agreed to take some of the refugees. But a year later, three of these countries were themselves under German control.

World War II begins

The Nazi noose was tightening around Europe. At daybreak on the morning of September 1, 1939, German armies invaded Poland, igniting World War II. A film explains just what the invasion meant. Polish Jews and other innocents were terror-

27

ized. Leadership of the country was taken over by the sadistic Nazi lawyer Hans Frank. Poland became the site of many new concentration camps, modeled after those that had existed in Germany for several years. These were the dumping grounds for Hitler's *Untermenschen*.

Not all the "inferior people" were shipped to Poland. Many of the insane or mentally ill were eliminated right in their home countries. An exhibit shows a bed from a "hospital" near Wiesbaden, Germany, where "patients" were strapped and then injected with a deadly dose of drugs. The haunting photo of a handicapped child, killed in this way, stares out at you from the wall. This was the start of Operation T-4, the order of September 1, 1939, that legalized euthanasia—mercy killing. In this way, thousands of people whom Hitler called "life unworthy of life" were quietly murdered.

In a darkened corner, away from the exhibits, stands a small tree stump, protected by a glass case. This lone stump was moved here from Palmiry, Poland, where it stood as the solitary sentinel at a mass grave. In the grave were buried dozens of Poles, murdered without cause by their German invaders. This is the end of the exhibits on the fourth floor of the Museum. And it marks the end of peace in Europe for the next six years.

4
BRIDGE TO THIRD FLOOR

HERNE, HERSFELD, HESSDORF . . .

Just three weeks after the invasion of Poland, a new law ordered Jews across the Reich to leave their homes and move into special sections of cities. These were the ghettos—often located in the very worst parts of town. Quickly these areas became overcrowded, filthy, and disease-ridden. Walls or barbed-wire fences enclosed the ghettos, and most residents were not allowed to leave without a permit. Where the ghetto was divided by a main road or trolley track, Jews had to cross from one section to the other over specially built bridges, since they were not allowed to mix with "Aryans" or use public streets and sidewalks.

During a tour of the Museum, visitors cross two bridges that connect the Museum towers, just as Jews crossed bridges from one part of the ghetto to another. Unlike the ghetto bridges, however, those at the Museum are enclosed by glass panels. The clear glass admits a refreshing light, a momentary but pleasant relief from the darkened exhibit halls. Etched on the panels of the bridge leading from the fourth to the third floor are the names of European towns and *shtetls* (Jewish villages) that were attacked or destroyed by the Nazis. Herne, Hersfeld, Hessdorf—more

One of five glass bridges connecting the towers of the main Museum building. This is the fourth-floor bridge, on which are etched the names of towns attacked or destroyed by the Nazis.

than five thousand communities are listed.

Across the bridge is an educational center filled with television monitors and computer terminals. Here visitors can select from a number of instructional programs about the Holocaust. One of the programs is called "American Responses to the Jewish Refugee Problem." Newspaper headlines and newsreel pictures from the late 1930s make clear that many Americans—and the American government—knew about the persecution of the Jews as early as 1938 but did little or nothing to stop it.

Towering ahead in the next room is an astounding display of photographs, mounted on four walls and reaching three stories high. This is the Tower of Faces—photographs taken in the *shtetl* of Eishishok, near the city of Vilna, Lithuania. Some 6,000 photos of daily life in the *shtetl* were gathered by one of its former residents, Yaffa Sonenson Eliach. Yaffa was four years old when the 3,400 Jews of her town were executed by a special division of Hitler's SS in September 1941. She was one of just 29 people to survive. As you stand there, looking up at this huge tower of faces, made from photos that might well be in your own family's albums, the Holocaust becomes very real. This was not a war between nations or armies. It was the intentional murder of innocent people just like you.

5

THIRD FLOOR

THE
FINAL SOLUTION,
1940-1944

Hitler expands his Reich

Despite their pleas to remain neutral, the Low Countries—Belgium, Luxembourg, and the Netherlands—were attacked by German forces just eight months after the capture of Poland. Helen Waterford and her husband, Siegfried Wohlfarth, whose stories are told on the ID cards, were among the Jews who had fled to the Netherlands from Germany..They were living in Amsterdam on the night the Nazis invaded:

> During the early morning hours of May 10, 1940, Hell broke loose. We were awakened by the roar and flak of hundreds of airplanes. The radio announced the invasion by German paratroopers who had parachuted into the country at 3 A.M. Some friends came over during the night. Together we did not feel so helpless, but we did realize that Holland was powerless to stop this wave that would eventually swallow us all. There were serious discussions of suicide; we knew how desperate our situation was.

Also living in Amsterdam that night was Anne Frank, whose family Helen and Siegfried had known back in Frankfurt, Germany. The Museum's third floor opens with a display about Anne's life, showing photos of her and of the family's hiding place, where Anne wrote her diary. *Through her life*, a Museum sign says, *Anne Frank has become an emblem of lost potential.*

The ghettos

As you enter the main exhibit area, the surface underfoot changes to rough, bumpy cobblestones that form an unpredictable path. The room is darker and the walkway seems narrower. Suddenly the cobblestones end and the floor changes to wooden planks. A crude handrail of rough-cut boards strung with wire keeps visitors on the path. This is the ghetto.

On the wall is a register, a board once used to record each ghetto resident's number. Hanging from the ceiling are TV monitors showing films and still pictures from inside the ghettos. Most of the photos were taken by German guards, to show the buildings or the type of work the people were forced to perform. But some were taken by ghetto residents themselves, and the expressions on the faces in these photos clearly show the pain, fear, and hopelessness that each person felt.

Throughout this exhibit are artifacts and visual reminders of the squalid life in the ghettos, where two million Jews and eight thousand Gypsies were confined. By the summer of 1942, there were more than 400 ghettos in German-occupied eastern Europe. The Nazis' "model" ghetto was Theresien-stadt, in Czechoslovakia, where 140,937 Jews were shipped. Among them was Ruth Reiser, thirteen years old when the Germans invaded her hometown of Prague.

To convince the world that conditions at Theresienstadt were more than adequate for its residents, the SS invited representatives from the International Red Cross to visit the ghetto in 1944. The Museum exhibit explains that prior to the Red Cross's visit, the Nazis built a bank, a café, shops, and schools. None of these were ever used, of course; they were constructed simply to impress the Red Cross representatives.

One of the striking artifacts in this part of the Museum is a detailed scale model of the Lodz Ghetto in Poland, showing all the streets and bridges. It was made by resident Leon Jacobson, who, fearing that his work would be discovered by Nazi guards, buried his model in the ground, inside a violin-shaped case. After the war, his brothers found it in the rubble and returned it to him.

Across the way is a replica of the largest remaining section of wall that once enclosed Poland's Warsaw Ghetto. The replica is cast directly from the original wall. Standing before it is what an official of the Museum calls "one of its most important artifacts"—a rusted old milk can in which resident Emanuel Ringelblum stored records of daily life in the Warsaw Ghetto. Ringelblum was a historian who realized that someday the world would want to know exactly what had gone on in this hell on Earth. To hide his papers from the Nazis, he stored them in milk cans that he buried in the dirt beneath the ghetto. The first one was discovered one year after the war ended, in 1946. The second, which is displayed at the Museum, was recovered in 1950. Ringelblum's archives had survived; he had not.

There are remains of a stained glass window from a syn-

One of the milk cans that held archives from the Warsaw Ghetto

agogue in Cracow, Poland. A cemetery gate with a rusted Star of David is on display from the Polish town of Tarnow. Nearby, a manhole cover stands as a grisly reminder of one of the few means of escape from the ghettos.

Not many people escaped successfully; those who did had a careful plan of their route, a source of money, and a place to go. For prospective escapees, the sewer system was a vital part of the route. The Museum's manhole cover illustrates the story of a few daring prisoners who got out of the Warsaw Ghetto by crawling through the city's sewers. Those who did escape sometimes hid in nearby forests. Others found Polish families who were willing to take them in, despite the threat of death to all if they were discovered.

There were two other ways to "escape" the ghetto. You could be deported, shipped away to a concentration camp. Or you could die. One out of every ten residents of the Warsaw Ghetto died during 1941. One out of two—half of all inhabitants—died in Theresienstadt during 1942.

A solution to the "Jewish problem"

Visitors now arrive at a bank of TV monitors, positioned down behind cement walls so young children cannot see them. Their screens show pictures of the grotesque killing methods used by the *Einsatzgruppen*, the Nazis' "Special Action Groups." One method was mass shootings, where victims were lined up along the edge of a pit so their bodies would fall where they could be covered quickly and easily. A sign says that one-quarter of the Jews who perished in the Holocaust were shot to death. The *Einsatzgruppen* also had mobile killing vans, equipped for murdering several people at a time. A poisonous gas was pumped into the backs of these vans, killing its victims immediately.

But these methods were inefficient. If the Nazis hoped to accomplish their goal of genocide, they needed a faster means of killing. Thousands were dying in the ghettos and concentration camps, but they were not dying fast enough. To address the problem, a conference was held on January 20, 1942, in the Berlin suburb of Wannsee. Here the SS outlined a plan it called the "Final Solution to the Jewish Question." The Final Solution was a blueprint for mass murder. It called for special extermination camps to be set up in Poland. Unlike concentration camps, where prisoners worked as slaves for the Reich, these were death camps; their sole purpose was to destroy on a grand scale—thousands of people a day.

Moving past the monitors, you come to a wrenching display of pitiful homemade weapons with which the Warsaw Ghetto residents fought the SS during the spring of 1943. Knowing that they were soon to die, a group of ghetto dwellers called the ZOB (Polish for "Jewish Fighting Organization") prepared for battle. They smuggled what few weapons they could into the ghetto and built more from bits of broken and rusted metal. On April 19, when the SS arrived to ship people to concentration camps and death camps, the ZOB was ready. Valiantly the Jews fought with their crude weapons, holding out for nearly a month, and in the end dying heroes' deaths. The date chosen for the dedication and opening of the United States Holocaust Memorial Museum—the week of April 19, 1993—marked the fiftieth anniversary of the heroic Warsaw Ghetto uprising.

Deportation

Directly ahead on your pathway is a chilling intersection. To the right, you see the end of an actual boxcar that was used for deporting victims to the ghettos and camps. In the distance on the left is a barrack where prisoners were housed in the camps. As you approach the boxcar, a film shows scenes from the transit camps—temporary places where the SS brought their victims to await deportation to concentration camps or ghettos.

One of the largest transit camps was Westerbork, in the Netherlands, where Tommy Pfeffer and his family were sent when they were discovered by the Gestapo. Here Tommy celebrated his seventh birthday, on November 22, 1943. Shortly after, his family was shipped to the Theresienstadt Ghetto to face a winter of fear, bitter cold, and starvation.

A boxcar used to deport victims to concentration camps sits on railroad tracks from the Treblinka death camp. On the right, at the end of the car, is a guard tower.

Deportees had no choice; they were forced by the hundreds into boxcars. But Museum visitors who prefer not to walk through the boxcar can take an alternate path around it. Those who walk through are stunned by the thought of 100 or more people crowded into this small space. The car is barren inside; there is no seating, no water or toilet facilities, no heating or cooling system. High on each wall is a small, window-like rectangle, but rarely were these opened. Several boxcars made up each train, carrying a total of one thousand to two thousand people. Because of their heavy loads, the trains moved slowly, averaging 30 miles per hour. The trip from Westerbork to the death camps in Poland took approximately three days and nights.

Victims knew little about where they were headed or the horrors that awaited them, because no one had yet come back from the camps to tell the terrible truth. The Nazis were careful to keep the deportees unaware so they would not panic and create chaos. They encouraged them to pack warm clothing, saying that they were going to be "resettled" in the east. Some were told that they would be sent to "family camps," where mothers could care for the children while men worked for the Reich. Of course, it was all a lie.

The selection process

Visitors exit the boxcar onto a selection ramp, like those at the extermination camps of Auschwitz, Treblinka, Sobibor, Majdanek, Belzec, and Chelmno. Thrown on the ground beside the car are piles of luggage, on which the owners had been ordered to write their names. This was a trick by the Nazis to make prisoners think their luggage would be delivered to them in their barracks.

Wall panels explain how the selection process took place on the ramps at the death camps. Here it was decided who would live and who would die. The most famous of the many Nazis to perform the selections was Dr. Josef Mengele, who greeted arrivals at Auschwitz. As the long line of new prisoners paraded by him, Mengele would simply flick his left thumb or his right thumb to indicate which line a person should join. One line went immediately to the gas chambers to be killed. The other was spared temporarily to do slave labor in the camp.

On the wall ahead are "mug shots" of prisoners in uniform. Mingled with the photos are many different uniform patches, reminding visitors that Jews were not Hitler's only victims. Each group of "undesirables" wore special symbols on their clothing to indicate what type of prisoners they were: Gypsy, homosexual, communist, etc. Jews wore a yellow cloth star on their uniforms; for Jehovah's Witnesses, the patch was a purple triangle; homosexuals had pink triangles, political prisoners red. Each inmate had a number which was often printed beside the symbol on the uniform patch. The use of numbers rather than names was one of the many devices the Nazis used to make their victims feel subhuman.

The next display is a horrifying reminder that the Holocaust happened to ordinary people, just like you. Piled in a tall heap is a huge collection of combs, toothbrushes, scissors, and silverware—personal items taken from each of the doomed prisoners as they arrived at the camps. On the opposite wall is a stark reminder that handicapped people were killed upon arrival, for here are piled leg braces, special support shoes, crutches, and artificial limbs—obviously of no further use to their owners.

Life—and death—in the camps

You pass now under the replica of the metal gate at Auschwitz, with its promising message: *Arbeit Macht Frei*, "Work Makes You Free." This was, of course, a gross and cruel untruth. On the left looms the barrack that was visible earlier. It comes from Birkenau, one section of the huge Auschwitz

40

Replica of the sign at the entrance to Auschwitz, telling prisoners that by working hard they will earn their freedom.

camp. Auschwitz was one of two camps that were both a labor camp *and* an extermination camp. Birkenau was the killing center at Auschwitz.

Before entering the barrack, you pause for a few minutes in the audio theater across from it. Seated in near darkness on stone benches, you can hear the quiet, tape-recorded voices of Auschwitz survivors, describing life in the camp. Helen Waterford tells how, upon arrival, women with children were separated from those without. "You think, 'Oh, they are with the children; they will be taken care of.' That's what we all thought." But in reality, the line of women with children went immediately to the gas chambers to be killed. Older teenagers could be used as slave laborers for the Reich. But there was simply no place for pregnant women or mothers with young

Photo 7 of 9

Hungarian Jews on their way to the gas chambers. Auschwitz-Birkenau, Poland, 1944.

Photo on a computer screen in the Wexner Learning Center shows Hungarian Jewish mothers and children on their way to the gas chambers at Auschwitz-Birkenau.

children at Auschwitz. Only if the mothers separated themselves from their children did they stand a chance of living.

Prisoners who were not selected for death were made to stand naked in line, waiting to have their heads shaved, get tattooed with a prison number, and be issued some ragged piece of clothing. But the most important item they received, says survivor Michael Vogel, was a round bowl. "This bowl was the lifeblood of your being. First of all, without it you couldn't get the meager rations that we got. And second, the bathroom facilities were almost nonexistent. . . ." Prisoners used their food bowls for toilet purposes.

The voices go on, telling their horrific stories of daily life in Auschwitz. Survivors watched their comrades being beaten for "crimes" as small as wrapping a blanket around themselves in winter. For several hours every morning and evening, they were forced to stand in frigid temperatures or kneel on the rock-covered ground with their hands in the air, while guards counted every prisoner. Even the dead had to be brought from the barracks and put on the ground so the count would be correct.

"Some people could take it and some people could not," says the voice of Sam Goldberg. "Some people just gave it up. . . . I didn't want to give up. I didn't want to give them a chance to kill me. No way."

You enter the barrack now, where rough wooden bunks line one entire wall. From five to ten people shared each bunk, some working while others slept. Sometimes prisoners were given blankets, but they were soon stolen or infested with lice.

A three-tiered bunk where prisoners slept stands in an actual barrack, moved to the Museum from Auschwitz-Birkenau.

Near the barren bunks is a display of brown enamel bowls, like those described by Michael Vogel. A sign says that 405,000 people were registered—given tattoo numbers—at Auschwitz. But the great majority of arrivals were not registered, for nearly all the young, the old, and the sick were sent at once to the gas chambers. Nearly one and a quarter million people were killed at Auschwitz-Birkenau. Of those, one million were Jews; ten thousand to twenty thousand were Soviet prisoners of war; twenty thousand were Gypsies; and tens of thousands were Poles. The Germans considered most Polish-speaking people to be racially inferior, good only for slave labor, and treated them like the Jews, Gypsies, and other "undesirables."

Along one wall is a pile of stone, taken from a quarry at Mauthausen, one of the first concentration camps built in Austria. As the rock was removed from the quarry, prisoners were made to haul it in their arms or on their backs up "the stairs of death." The average life span for quarry workers at Mauthausen was one and a half to three months—if they were not shot sooner by the SS.

The death factories

In the center of the barrack stands a model of a gas chamber door, cast from an actual door at Majdanek, another death camp in Poland. Doors like these sealed the rooms where dozens of naked prisoners were led for what they were told would be a shower. But instead, through a hole in the roof of the chamber, guards poured Zyklon B, the infamous crystals that released a deadly poison gas when they hit the floor, killing their victims within minutes. Built into the chamber

44

door is a small peephole through which guards could look to tell when the prisoners were dead. An actual can of Zyklon B sits nearby, a grim reminder of how many people's fates were sealed when these doors were closed and the crystals poured through the roof.

Perhaps the most chilling display in the Museum is a scale model of Crematorium II, one of the four killing centers at Auschwitz-Birkenau. Polish artist Mieczyslaw Stobierski made this huge model from a white plaster material. A cut-away view shows a long line of people moving from ground level down into the undressing room of the killing center. To

A model of Polish sculptor Mieczyslaw Stobierski's crematorium, showing roughly how the bodies were burned

keep the prisoners calm, guards told them to remember where they put their clothes, so they could claim them later. But of course there was no "later."

The model next shows prisoners heading into the "shower" room. On the roof, a guard is pouring Zyklon B crystals into a grate. In the next scene, the victims are dead and fellow prisoners are hauling their bodies to the ovens to be cremated. Along the way the workers stop to shave the women's heads for valuable hair and check the bodies for gold dental fillings. A sign near the model says that Crematorium II had fifteen ovens, each capable of holding three to four bodies. In this way, one thousand bodies a day were burned— at this single crematorium alone. Prisoners who were assigned to load bodies into the ovens sometimes saw the faces of their own dead relatives or friends, but for fear of being killed themselves, they could show no signs of grief.

As visitors leave the barrack and this horrific display, two wall panels explain why the United States government refused to bomb the Auschwitz extermination camp. Bombing would have destroyed the equipment of mass murder, thereby saving hundreds of thousands of lives. But the U.S. government decided that such a move would require too many planes and other military equipment that was critical to fighting the war. The government claimed it was also worried that bombing would irritate the Germans into taking even fiercer revenge on their victims—if that were possible. And so the death camps were ignored, left untouched to continue their abominable work, while just a few miles away, targets of greater interest to the military were bombed again and again.

One of those prisoners who might have been saved

was Tommy Pfeffer. On May 18, 1944, Tommy was deported to Auschwitz from the Theresienstadt Ghetto. He managed to stay alive in Auschwitz for nearly two months, but he never celebrated his eighth birthday. On July 11, 1944, Tommy was gassed.

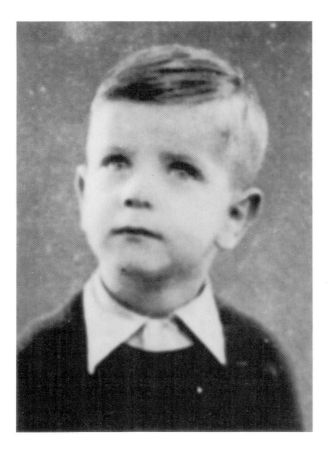

Thomas Pfeffer

6

BRIDGE TO SECOND FLOOR

HEINRICH,
HELEN, HERI . . .

Your mind is having a hard time accepting what your eyes have seen. You try to comprehend the evil you have witnessed as you cross another glass bridge, into the tower leading to the second floor. The glass on this bridge is etched not with the names of towns but with the first names of victims—people who perished in the Holocaust. *Heinrich, Helen, Heri . . .* the list seems endless.

Even before you emerge from the bridge, you sense the odor of leather—not new, fresh leather, but worn leather with a definite human smell. In a huge bin in front of you lie 4,000 shoes, styles from the 1930s and 1940s. Their owners are dead, gassed in the killing centers of Poland. From just two of the death camps alone, Auschwitz-Birkenau and Majdanek, nearly 300,000 pairs of shoes were taken from victims and given to German civilians or slave laborers in the concentration camps. Many times that number were taken from victims at other camps. The smell of the shoes, as well as a haunting vision of the people who wore them, stays fixed in your mind.

Along the wall is a huge photo of human hair—piles of it, bags of it—shaved from the heads of victims and turned into felt, a crude cloth from which the Nazis made stockings

A small section of the sea of shoes, taken by Nazi guards from prisoners at the Majdanek death camp in Poland for their submarine crew members and railroad workers. Another group of photos tells the story of the tattoo process and how it varied from camp to camp. The display shows how prisoners were registered with numbers and where on the body the tattoos were placed.

As you turn away from this bizarre scene, you come face-to-face with the tools of death. Before you are replicas of two crematorium ovens, just like those used in the extermination camps to burn the victims' bodies. So hot were the fires in these ovens, and so constantly were they in use, that steel bands had to be strapped around them to reinforce the bricks.

To the left is a table where bodies were placed before cremation for removal of gold dental fillings and other valuables. On the right sits the frame of a large truck, used to haul bodies from the gas chambers to the ovens. Sometimes the frames served as grates, when the bodies were burned in outdoor fire pits.

The practical, organized fashion in which the Nazis set about the process of mass murder is hard to comprehend. How could human beings do this to each other? you ask yourself. How could they kill so callously, in such a matter-of-fact way? As Elie Wiesel has warned, the Museum does not answer these questions—because there are no answers.

It is a relief, at last, to be delivered out of the death factory, into the lower level of the Tower of Faces. Sadness replaces horror, as you stare at this sea of photos of innocent faces. In the *shtetl* of Eishishok, a sign says, "900 years of Jewish life came to an end in two days." If you had been living there in 1941, you would have been killed, too.

7

SECOND FLOOR

THE AFTERMATH, 1944-PRESENT

The title of the second-floor displays—"After-math"—implies that the end is near. By 1944, the Nazi death machine was beginning to fail. There were serious cracks in the foundation of the Reich. Germany was on its way to losing World War II. But all this remained unknown to the millions of prisoners still held in the camps. For them, death was ever present. The only future they knew was staying alive from minute to hour.

Eighteen-year-old Ruth Reiser was among those fighting for her life. Late in 1944, Ruth had been deported to Auschwitz from the Theresienstadt Ghetto. In the desperate hope of getting out of Auschwitz, she stood in a long line of women who were rumored to be going to a labor camp. "I managed to stand near the front of the column of 1,000 women," says the story on her I.D. card. Although inmates never knew just what would happen to them in camps, usually it was a good sign to be counted out for a particular group. Victims selected for the gas chambers were rarely counted.

Ruth was hopeful that being near the head of this line of one thousand women meant that she would be counted for the group going to the labor camp. "Then a command of 'Turn

About!' dashed my hopes. I ended up at the back of the line with those to be gassed." Ruth and her fellow inmates feared that after the guards had counted out the right number for the labor camp, those left over would be killed.

"Nobody slept that night as, expecting to die, we waited in front of the crematorium." But when the new day dawned, luck was on Ruth's side. She was put into the labor transport and sent to Lenzing, a subcamp of the infamous Mauthausen camp in Austria. For a while longer, Ruth would have the chance to live.

The righteous among nations
Had it not been for small numbers of people whose con-sciences kept them from looking the other way, even more

A fishing boat, used to transport Jews from Denmark to neutral Sweden, stands at the entrance to the Museum's second floor.

victims would have died in the Holocaust. Unlike other European countries that were under Nazi control, the entire nation of Denmark stubbornly refused to let its Jews be persecuted. Because Denmark cared about its Jews and respected them like all other citizens, 90 percent of its Jewish population was saved.

The Danes defied the Nazis by secretly ferrying Jews in small fishing boats to the neutral country of Sweden. "We must obey God before we obey man," the head of the Lutheran church reminded his followers. One of the fishing boats that ferried thousands of Danish Jews to safety is displayed on the second floor of the Holocaust Museum.

This is the floor of resisters and rescuers—those "Righteous Gentiles," as the Jews call them, who were brave enough or concerned enough to defy the evil of the Nazi regime. Three young resisters, who called themselves the White Rose, operated at the University of Munich. Hans Scholl, his sister Sophie, and a friend, Christopher Probst—all in their early twenties—were outraged by the loss of their freedom under the Nazis and by reports they were hearing of concentration camps and mass murders. The group called on the German people to resist the Nazis in any way they could. Between late 1942 and early 1943, the White Rose passed out leaflets calling for the "renewal of the mortally wounded German spirit." In just a short time, the three were arrested, tried by a Nazi court, and sentenced to death. On February 22, 1943, they were beheaded. Hans went to his death crying, "Long live freedom!"

Across from the White Rose exhibit is a huge wall bearing the names of hundreds of rescuers from several countries

The White Rose display on the Museum's second floor tells the heroic story of three young resisters in Munich, Germany.

in Europe. These were ordinary people, laborers and house-wives who—at great risk to themselves and their families—defied the Nazis and helped the persecuted people. Many of them belonged to underground movements, which were secret organizations that helped Jews find homes, food, or a means of escape. The Wall of Rescuers is arranged by country, the longest list belonging to the Netherlands.

Several of the Righteous from France were from Le

Chambon, the village that became a safe haven for 5,000 Jews, among them many children. The rescue movement was started by André Trocmé, the pastor of the local church, and his wife, who took fleeing Jews into their home when the Nazis overran France in 1940. Soon their neighbors joined the effort, and in time the entire town was hiding Jews, even after the pastor was arrested.

Partisans and resisters

It wasn't just the Gentiles who resisted; a number of Jews also fought back. Many of them joined partisan groups of guerrilla fighters who lived on the run in the forests of eastern Europe. Often the partisans were escapees from ghettos; the Vilna Avengers, for example, were veterans of the Vilna Ghetto in Lithuania.

The partisans' goal was to wreak havoc on the Nazi system, wherever and however they could. They stole or destroyed German guns and ammunition; they broke into warehouses where food coupons were stored and stole them for the people living underground. They destroyed trains and train tracks, and attacked small Nazi guard units. Partisans also performed their acts of sabotage in the cities of western Europe. But here, without the protection of the forests, they had to use even greater caution to avoid being caught.

Although they stood little chance of succeeding, Jews in three of the death camps also fought back. At Auschwitz-Birkenau, Treblinka, and Sobibor, the prisoners planned and carried out uprisings. Tomasz (Toivi) Blatt, a sixteen-year-old Polish Jew, was one of those involved in the escape from Sobibor on October 14, 1943. He tells his story on an ID card:

During the revolt, prisoners streamed to one of the holes cut in the barbed-wire fence. They weren't about to wait in line; there were machine guns shooting at us. They climbed on the fence and just as I was halfway through, it collapsed, trapping me underneath. This saved me. The first ones through hit mines [which exploded and killed them]. When most of them were through, I slid out of my coat, which was hooked on the fence, and ran till I reached the forest.

Tomasz (Toivi) Blatt

Tomasz was one of the fortunate few who made it to safety. He went into hiding and worked for the Polish underground until the end of the war.

The death marches
By the end of 1944, the Nazis knew they were in grave danger of losing World War II. This made them all the more determined not to lose the war against the Jews. From the east, Russian armies advanced across Po- land, headed for Germany's capital, Berlin. Lying in their paths were the six massive extermination camps and hundreds of smaller concentration camps of the Third Reich.

Thomas Bürgenthal

Nazi leaders wanted no witnesses left to tell of their horrific crimes. And so, as Russian troops moved closer, the Nazis rounded up hundreds of thousands of prisoners who could still walk and forced them to march. In the depths of the frigid Polish winter, the weak and starving victims were marched to concentration camps in Ger-many. Huge numbers died along the way. Ten-year-old Thomas Bürgenthal was one of those on the forced march from Auschwitz in January 1945. An ID card tells his story:

> We were marched out—children at the front. Day one was a 10-hour march and tiring; we began to lag. Stragglers were shot, so two boys and I devised a way to rest as we walked: We'd run to the front of the column, then walk slowly or stop until the rear of the column reached us. Then we would run ahead again.

Altogether, 66,000 prisoners were deported from Auschwitz on this death march, which lasted three days. A quarter of them died along the way. Thomas was one of only three children to survive.

It did the Germans little good to move the prisoners into Germany, for by spring, British and American armies were heading toward Berlin from the west. On a panel of TV monitors, visitors watch newsreel films of the first Allied soldiers entering the camps on liberation day. What the soldiers found so disgusted and enraged them that they lost control. At the Dachau camp in Germany, American soldiers attacked the SS guards and then allowed the inmates to take out their revenge as well.

American army General George Patton was leading the troops that liberated the German camp of Buchenwald on April 11, 1945. So upset was he by what he saw that he ordered his men to go into a nearby town and bring back one thousand German civilians. He wanted them to walk through the camp and see for themselves what had gone on in their own backyards. Patton's men, equally angered by the scene in Buchenwald, brought back two thousand civilians instead.

British troops liberated Bergen-Belsen, where Anne Frank had been a prisoner. (Anne, like several thousand other inmates, had died of typhus in the final weeks before liberation.) Still lying about the camp in the sun were thousands of unburied bodies. Of the 60,000 prisoners alive on liberation day, 14,000 would die in the days immediately following, and another 14,000 over the next few weeks.

Justice

The world could not believe the stories it was finally hearing of the horror in Nazi Europe. At last, but far too late, people awoke to the monstrosity of the crimes that had been committed. On May 7, 1945, Germany surrendered; World War II was over in Europe. Within two weeks, plans were made for the trials of top Nazis accused of crimes against humanity and other war crimes. The ancient German city of Nuremberg, once the site of spectacular Nazi Party conventions but now a mass of war-torn rubble, was chosen as the location for the trials. They began on November 20, 1945, and lasted nearly a year.

Panels, pictures, and films explain the fate of the demons who crafted the "Final Solution." Of the twenty-two high-ranking Nazis on trial at Nuremberg, twelve were sentenced to death, three received life imprisonment, and four got shorter prison terms. Three were found not guilty and set free. Adolf Hitler did not have to stand trial. On April 30, 1945, as Berlin was about to be captured, Hitler and his wife of one day, Eva Braun, went into the Führer's underground bunker and committed suicide.

The Museum displays give you the feeling of being present at the Nuremberg trials. You can picture Rudolf Hess, the number-three man in the Nazi Party, reading novels and sleeping while the court was in session. Hess was sentenced to life in prison, which he served, finally committing suicide in 1987.

Hermann Göring, head of the *Luftwaffe* (the German air force) and organizer of the Gestapo—the second most powerful man in Nazi Germany—was photographed laughing in the courtroom, apparently finding some humor in a translator's mistake. He is said to have hissed, "Swine!" during the testimony of one witness he particularly disliked. Göring's scorn finally turned to fear when he was sentenced to death by hanging. But in the end, he cheated the hangman by committing suicide shortly before his hour of execution.

Another exhibit tells the fate of one of the most notorious Nazis who wasn't tried at Nuremberg. This was Adolf Eichmann, a lieutenant colonel in the SS and the man in charge of coordinating the trains that carried victims to concentration and death camps. At the end of the war, Eichmann escaped to Argentina, where he lived under a false identity until 1960. That year, Israeli agents captured him and brought him to trial in Israel. He was found guilty and was executed in 1962.

Over the years, other Nazis who lived in hiding were finally discovered and put on trial. As recently as 1993, an Israeli court acquitted John Demjanjuk, who was accused of being "Ivan the Terrible," the fearsome guard at the Treblinka death camp. Many Jews around the world were outraged when he was freed from the charges against him, and they demanded a retrial. But because Israeli prosecutors lacked evidence to solidly convict him, a judge ruled against a retrial and Demjanjuk was returned to the United States, where he had been living for many years.

Although there are few wartime criminals still alive today, dedicated groups of Nazi hunters continue to pursue them in the hope of seeing justice done.

Rebuilding shattered lives

Bringing Nazi leaders to trial did little to ease the burden faced by survivors at the end of the war. How do you pick up the pieces of a devastated life and begin again? All across the ravaged continent of Europe people were scattered, completely separated from their homes and families. Ruth Reiser, now nineteen, returned to her hometown of Prague, Czechoslovakia, after it was liberated by American troops—only to find that she was the sole surviving member of her family.

From a labor camp in Czechoslovakia, survivor Helen

Waterford set out across Europe hoping to find her daughter, Doris. Three years earlier, when Doris was five, Helen and her husband had given up the child to total strangers in the Dutch city of Amsterdam, hoping that she would survive, even if they did not. After more than a month of travel through the bombed-out ruins of Germany, Helen arrived in the Netherlands to learn that Doris was alive. She had been taken in by a Righteous Gentile couple who cared for her as their own daughter.

Thousands of other children who had managed to survive now faced life as orphans because both their parents had died in the Holocaust. Some found relatives to care for them in their own home region. Others, like Thomas Bürgenthal, faced moving to the United States where an aunt or uncle they had never met would, they hoped, take them in.

Slowly, you head upward along a ramp. Your descent through the Museum and the hell of the Holocaust is nearly over. And yet a force seems to pull you back, begging you not to stop looking—yet. Projected onto a small screen surrounded by antique toys and small-size, old-fashioned clothes are the haunting faces of children. Some are the faces of those like Doris, who were put into hiding to escape the Nazis. Others are the faces of kids who, like Thomas Bürgenthal, suffered in the camps and death chambers. Lining the walls of the ramp are drawings done by children when they were prisoners in the ghettos and concentration camps. Some of the artists survived; others became part of the one and one half million children who perished in the Holocaust.

At the top of the ramp is a small theater showing an eighty-minute documentary film. Here, visitors can listen to the voices and watch the faces of some of those who survived the Holocaust. As they tell their terrible stories, many of the survivors cry openly; one is completely unemotional.

The only person in the film who is not a Holocaust survivor is Kurt Klein, who was a lieutenant with the Fifth U.S. Infantry Division during the liberation of the camps. Amid the devastation, Klein approached a young woman, Gerda Weissmann, who was starving but still alive.

"May I see the other ladies?" he asked her.

Ladies! she remembers thinking. He probably doesn't know . . . I must tell him.

"We are Jews," she confessed in a small voice.

"So am I," he answered, obviously shaken to consider what his fate might have been had he stayed in his native Germany, rather than escaping to the United States.

Out of the hatred and hellfire of the Holocaust, it was possible for love to grow. The survivor and the serviceman returned to the United States and were married—as happy an ending as is possible in this overpowering film.

Before you, as you exit the theater, you see the Hall of Remembrance. This is a place for reflection, where visitors can contemplate all they have witnessed inside the Museum's walls. But before you visit this quiet spot, there is one more exhibit to see.

8

FIRST FLOOR

REMEMBER
THE
CHILDREN

You return to the Hall of Witness, where our tour began, reflecting on all the evil and sadness you have seen in these few short hours. It is clear now why the Museum begs visitors to bear witness. Unless people understand how and why the Holocaust happened, such evil will have the chance to reign again.

What you have just witnessed on the three exhibition floors of the Museum is not recommended for children under eleven years old. Although the exhibits and most of the photos are not explicitly gruesome, the tragedy and inhumanity is too harsh for very young minds to comprehend.

Still, education is an important aim of the Museum. Its founders want children to know about the tragedy of the Holocaust, and to understand that it happened to real people like themselves. After all, the "Final Solution" did not spare children under age eleven.

To help younger visitors comprehend the Holocaust, the Museum has organized an exhibition titled "Remember the Children: Daniel's Story." It is located just off the Hall of Witness, across from the information desk. Daniel was not a real boy. But his story is drawn from the experiences of many children who did face the horror of the Hitler years. The time is 1933 and the place is Frankfurt, Germany, where six-year-old Daniel lives with his mother, father, and sister, Erika. His family owns a store in the city. You enter Daniel's exhibit by pushing back a heavy curtain—a reminder that you are entering "a time ago."

✡ ✡ ✡

DANIEL'S STORY

"Have you ever been punished for something you didn't do?" Daniel's voice asks as he introduces you to his family and his town. If you have, you know how the Jewish children of Germany felt when the Nazis took over their country.

Against a background of painted murals, a projector flashes films of happy children in pre-Nazi Germany. Small signs throughout the exhibit tell you what you are about to see, and suggest things for you to do along the way.

In happy times

Daniel invites you into his home, a neat, well-kept house, with his bicycle parked outside. For his birthday, his father gave him a diary. Every day he records in it what happens to him and to his family. On the wall are pages from the diary, enlarged so visitors can read them easily.

Inside Daniel's home you hear laughter and the happy voices of his mother and his sister, Erika. The house is cheery and clean, with nicely polished floors and photos of the family on the walls. A pair of skis stands by the door of the closet in the back hall. Daniel and Erika each have a shelf for their belongings. On Daniel's shelf are a soccer ball, a pair of skates, and toys like those that might be on your shelf in your home. *Look in the cabinet where mother kept the candlesticks,* says one of the small signs. *Visit Daniel's bedroom.*

His bedroom is a bright, pleasant place with a desk, a chair, and a bed made of pretty, light-colored wood. On a shelf is a model train locomotive and books, like those read by chil-

Daniel's diary sits on the desk in his bedroom.

dren all over Germany in the 1920s and 1930s. Open on his desk is a diary. Reading the first entry, you learn that Daniel got the diary for his birthday.

I want to write in it every day. I better keep it in my bedroom where my nosey sister Erika can't find it.

Scary changes

On January 20, 1933, Daniel's diary entry is not so pleasant.

Things are beginning to change. The Nazis are taking over more and more. Many people are following their ways. . . . Now some of my friends won't play with me because I'm Jewish. I feel awful.

As you walk through the hall in Daniel's house, there are windows you can lift to see just how things are beginning to change outside. A sign on a shop window says, DON'T BUY FROM JEWISH STORES. The word *JEW* is painted on the window of Daniel's family's store. At the swimming pool, a sign says NO JEWS ALLOWED, and at the skating rink, JEWS AND DOGS NOT PERMITTED.

Suddenly you hear the voice of an announcer, speaking from an arch-shaped, old-fashioned radio. "Attention! Attention!" It is 1938 and the announcer is reporting on a huge gathering in Munich, Germany. Nazi leaders have just addressed a crowd of faithful followers, telling them, "The Jews must be driven out!" A few days later, this entry appears in Daniel's diary:

NOVEMBER 10, 1938

   Dear Diary,

   Last night they burned our synagogue. The sky was red for hours. German firemen and Nazis

just stood around watching. It was the first time
I ever saw my father cry. It scared me to see father
like that.

Through the window of Daniel's home you can see the burning synagogue with its broken window. Glass lies on the ground next to a rock that broke it. Coats hang on a rack in the hallway of Daniel's house, ready to be thrown on quickly if the family should have to flee.

Everywhere along the paved streets of Daniel's town in the exhibit are signs of scary changes. A mural shows the scene of a pleasant park with an inviting, green park bench. Painted on it are the words *For Aryans Only*. A fence blocks your entrance, and a sign tells you that the park is closed to Jews. The only place where you may sit as you tour with Daniel is on a yellow bench outside the park marked *Only For Jews*. You sit for a moment, thinking what it must have been like to be a Jew in Germany in the 1930s.

In his diary Daniel writes,

They ruined our store! Nothing is safe for us any-
more. Everything is gone—my school, our home, our
store, our happy life. What will happen to us?

A German newspaper, for sale on a stand in the street in Daniel's town, announces the order to wear THE YELLOW STAR. Even though he doesn't want to, Daniel, like all Jews, must wear the star attached to his clothing, beginning in September 1941. The orders for making and wearing the star are posted on the newspaper stand:

1. Cut the star the size of your hand.
2. Color it YELLOW.
3. Outline it in BLACK.
4. Write JEW in black letters.
5. Sew it tightly to your clothes on the left side.
JEWS ARE FORBIDDEN to appear in public without the Yellow Star.

You look down the dark street. The sounds of happy voices have disappeared now. You feel very uneasy. Where is Daniel? An open suitcase shows you that he is getting ready to leave.

Daniel's suitcase is packed to leave.

Dear Diary,

Father and I used to play games with my train. Well, this is not a game! We are really being sent away.

I thought I would love to take a trip. Now, I don't want to leave home.

Daniel

OCTOBER 15, 1941

Dear Diary,

My mother says we must hurry with our suit-
cases. We are being sent to a ghetto far away. . . . My
father says thousands of Jews are being sent away.
Erika is crying. Will we ever see home again?

A small sign on a high gate says PUSH TO OPEN. Almost afraid to follow directions, you reach for the gate and nudge it reluctantly. It opens into a different world. This is the Lodz Ghetto, in Poland, where Daniel and his family have been deported.

Underneath your feet the road is rough cobblestone; the air feels colder. In the background, you hear children crying. People are arguing and yelling at one another. They speak in many different languages. The scene is confusing, chaotic. The Lodz Ghetto is obviously a very unhappy place.

Near a large mailbox, where all the people of the ghetto get their mail, is a note from Daniel's diary:

I wait for letters from friends. They are bits of hope
from the world outside the ghetto.

The cobblestone street leads you into Daniel's ghetto room. It is nothing like his bedroom back home. The walls are dirty and gray; a single lightbulb hangs from a long cord in the middle of the room. In the corner is a small, filthy sink. This is not Daniel's room alone; it is the bedroom, kitchen, bathroom, dining room, and living room all in one. He shares it with his mother, father, and Erika. His diary explains that

69

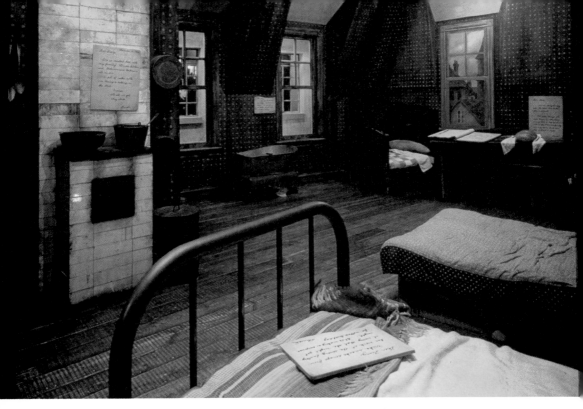

The single room in the Lodz ghetto where Daniel lived with his family

Erika hides behind a sheet so nobody can see her getting dressed. The crying of the children grows louder now. You want to leave, to go back to the pleasant life in Frankfurt, but you cannot. You must go on.

Taken away

A high, chain-link fence now looms before you. A short note from the diary says, *They are taking us away.*

On one side you see the end of a boxcar. In the other direction a dried grass pathway leads toward the entrance to a concentration camp. A film tells us what happened to Daniel here.

Upon arrival at the camp, he and his father were separated from his mother and Erika. Guards took away his diary, along with a medal for bravery that his father had received in World War I and that Daniel had carried with him all the way from home. Their heads were shaved and they were tattooed. All day, every day, Daniel was forced to work like a slave. At night he slept on a rough wooden bunk that he shared with eight men. Photos in the film show the faces of real children who were prisoners.

In a sad, quiet voice, Daniel tells what happened to his family. He and his father lived, and were liberated at the end of the war. But he never saw his mother again. Erika became one of the one and a half million children to die or be killed

The concentration camp to which Daniel and his family were deported

in the camps. "One and a half million . . . that's like a whole school disappearing every day for eight years," Daniel explains. "Remember my story," he pleads. "Remember the children."

You leave this part of Daniel's exhibit by pushing back a heavy curtain, as heavy as the sadness you are feeling. In the outer room you are invited to pick up one of the phones and hear questions and answers about what you have just seen. If you'd like to write down your thoughts, there are cards, pencils, and crayons. If you wish, you may drop your card in a special mailbox marked **mUSeum Mail.**

Many other children have put their thoughts on cards before saying good-bye to Daniel and his haunting story:

Dear Daniel, writes one 10-year-old girl, *I've never in life felt so sad about you and about the Holocaust. . . .*

And from a boy:

I hate to think how hard it must feel to lose your loving everyday Mother.

An unsigned card says:

When I saw this museum I realized this [the Holocaust] was real. . . .

If you have been able to put yourself in Daniel's place while visiting his exhibit, or in the place of any of the millions of Jewish children who lived during the Holocaust, you'll understand how the girl felt who left this message on her card:

People may be different, but one thing is the same: the human heart.

9

THE HALL
OF
REMEMBRANCE

A s you prepare to leave the United States Holocaust Memorial Museum, your mind is filled with confusing thoughts: horror at what you have seen happen to innocent people; anger at those who committed the terrible acts of brutality and at those who allowed this horror to happen; sadness for the victims. You need time to think, a place to go and reflect before you return to the outside world. This is the time to visit the Hall of Remembrance, the six-sided building adjacent to the main Museum.

A long ramp leads slowly up, around, and into the Hall. Overhead, a huge glass dome provides most of the building's light. The rest comes from tiny candles lit by visitors to remember victims of the Holocaust. On the night before the Museum opened, some six thousand Holocaust survivors gathered in Washington, D.C., to hold a candlelight vigil. Each tiny flame in that sea of six thousand candles represented one thousand Jewish people who perished in the Holocaust.

The Hall of Remembrance is a plain place, designed this way to let peoples' thoughts fill it as they choose. Visitors may sit on steps surrounding the large open space in the center of the Hall, to pray, to reflect, or simply to think. Special events

An eternal flame burns in the Hall of Remembrance above the vault filled with ashes gathered from each of the death camps. To the right and left are candles lit by visitors in memory of those who perished.

or ceremonies are sometimes held here in this amphitheater-like space.

On one side of the Hall of Remembrance is the eternal flame, lit by President Bill Clinton on opening day. Beneath the flame is a vault filled with dirt from each of the extermination camps. Mixed with the dirt are human ashes, the remains of just a few of the millions of victims of the Holocaust. On a wall behind the flame is a quotation from the biblical book of Deuteronomy:

> *Only guard yourself and guard your soul carefully, lest you forget the things your eyes saw, and lest these things depart your heart all the days of your life. And you shall make them known to your children and your children's children.*

TIME LINE OF
THE HOLOCAUST

January 30, 1933—Adolf Hitler is named chancellor of Germany.

May 10, 1933—In Berlin, Germany, Nazi storm troopers and university students burn thousands of books by authors who are considered "enemies of the state."

September 15, 1935—The Nuremberg laws, severely limiting the rights of Jews, go into effect in Germany. One of the new laws forbids marriage between Jews and so-called Aryan Germans. The Nazi swastika is made an official part of the German flag.

March 12, 1938—The *Anschluss* (reunification of the Germanic peoples) begins when German troops take over Austria without resistance.

July 6–15, 1938—Representatives from thirty-two countries meet at Evian, France, to discuss letting Jewish refugees enter their countries. Most have reasons why they cannot admit many Jews. Britain says it has no room for large groups; the U.S. agrees to take only a small number; Australia announces, "We have no real racial problem, and we are not desirous of importing one." Only Denmark, the Netherlands, and the Dominican Republic offer to change their existing laws to allow more Jews.

November 9–10, 1938—*Kristallnacht*, "the Night of Broken Glass." Across Germany, Nazis and their followers smash the windows of Jewish homes, stores, and synagogues. As a result of Kristallnacht, more than ninety Jews die; thirty thousand Jewish men are arrested and taken to concentration camps.

May 13, 1939—The ship *St. Louis* leaves port in Hamburg, Germany, with 936 passengers. Most of them are Jews, with permits to land in Cuba. But upon their arrival, Cuba refuses to admit them, and they are forced to return to Europe.

September 1, 1939—World War II begins, as Germany invades Poland at dawn.

May 20, 1940—The first prisoners are shipped to the Auschwitz concentration camp in Poland. By June, transports of several hundred people per day are arriving here.

November 15, 1940—A wall is completed around a section of the city of Warsaw, Poland, to be used as a ghetto. Jews themselves must pay for and build the wall.

September 19, 1941—All Jews older than six years are required to wear a yellow Star of David sewn on their clothing when they appear in public.

December 8, 1941—Chelmno, first of the extermination camps built solely for mass killing, goes into operation in Poland. Within nine months, three more death camps are opened and two concentration camps (Auschwitz-Birkenau and Majdanek) are expanded to include gas chambers and killing centers.

December 11, 1941—The United States and Germany declare war against each other.

January 20, 1942—A highly secret conference is held in the Berlin suburb of Wannsee. Reich security chief Reinhard Heydrich outlines plans for the "Final Solution to the Jewish Question." Although the word "killing" is never mentioned, it is clear that the Final Solution means genocide—mass murder of all Jewish people.

December 16, 1942—A Nazi decree orders all Gypsies in Europe to be deported to Auschwitz; 16,000 are murdered as soon as they arrive. By the end of the war, 200,000 of Europe's 700,000 Gypsies will have been killed by the Nazis.

April 19, 1943—The Warsaw Ghetto uprising begins.

October 14, 1943—Prisoners at the Sobibor death camp attempt to escape. About two hundred inmates make it to the safety of the nearby forests.

May–June 1944—Nearly 400,000 Hungarian Jews are murdered at Auschwitz-Birkenau.

January 17–23, 1945—As Russian armies move closer to liberating Auschwitz, the Nazis force inmates on a death march to other camps.

April 30, 1945—Adolf Hitler commits suicide.

May 7, 1945—Germany surrenders. World War II in Europe is over.

November 20, 1945—The trials of Nazi war criminals begin in the German city of Nuremberg.

FOR FURTHER READING

BOOKS

Ayer, Eleanor H. *Parallel Journey*. New York: Atheneum Publishers, 1994.

Berenbaum, Michael. *The World Must Know: The History of the Holocaust as Told in the United States Holocaust Memorial Museum*. Boston: Little, Brown, 1993.

Fry, Varian. *Assignment: Rescue*. New York: Scholastic, 1945, 1968.

Gilbert, Martin. *The Holocaust: A History of the Jews of Europe During the Second World War*. New York: Holt, Rinehart and Winston, 1985.

———. *The Macmillan Atlas of the Holocaust*. New York: Macmillan, 1982.

Goralski, Robert. *World War II Almanac, 1931–1945*. New York: Bonanza Books, 1984.

Hilberg, Raul. *The Destruction of the European Jews*. New York: Holmes & Meier, 1985.

Keller, Ulrich, ed. *The Warsaw Ghetto in Photographs*. New York: Dover Publications, 1984.

Levin, Nora. *The Holocaust: The Destruction of European Jewry, 1933–45*. New York: Thomas Y. Crowell, 1968.

Matas, Carol. *Daniel's Story*. New York: Scholastic, 1993.

Rogasky, Barbara. *Smoke and Ashes: The Story of the Holocaust*. New York: Holiday House, 1988.

Waterford, Helen. *Commitment to the Dead: One Woman's Journey Toward Understanding*. Frederick, Colo.: Renaissance House, 1987.

PERIODICALS

Allen, Henry. "Holocaust Museum Dedicated With Hope." *Washington Post*, April 23, 1993: A1, A14.

Bettelheim, Adriel. "A Place for Remembering." *Denver Post*, May 9, 1993: 1T, 3T.

Burchard, Hank. "The House of Inhumanity." *Washington Post Weekend*, April 23, 1993: 51–53.

Kernan, Michael. "A National Memorial Bears Witness to the Tragedy of the Holocaust." *Smithsonian*, April 1993: 50–63.

Kimmelman, Michael. "Holocaust Museum Dedicated in Payment to Dead." *New York Times*, April 23, 1993: A1, A24.

Morrow, Lance. "Never Forget." *Time*, April 26, 1993: 56–57.

Muschamp, Herbert. "Shaping a Monument to Memory." *New York Times*, April 11, 1993: section 2: 1, 32.

INDEX